For Simon,

Mirsad Solakovic *Russel*

THE BOY WHO SAID NOTHING

With warmest wishes
and I hope in life
you find a light of
happiness with
wisdom to love
People and different
nations,

1

I dedicate this book to my mum and dad who stood by me through all of the difficult times in my life. I would also like to thank the people who assisted my family during the war in Bosnia in 1992. I send my condolences to all victims of war including: the children, my relatives and the loyal citizens of Bosnia & Herzegovina.

We are all someone's children, someone's mother, father, and grandparent.

Love and care should blossom between all people the same way as it blossoms within a family.

Author

Fellow citizens of this world

Bosnia survived an atrocious war by fighting against the enemies who wanted her no more.

Her true sons gave their hearts, souls and blood for her to survive; doing whatever it took to keep the real invaders at bay.

One country, one nation, against itself it seems, where people who were once like brothers later acted as enemies.

The end result was somewhat unknown, where even the evil invaders could not recognise the purpose of their role.

This, unfortunately, we have seen before, and history continues to repeat itself for ever more.

I, too, am one of her sons, who will give my heart and soul to make sure that Bosnia does not have to re-live that darkness for even one more day.

This is why I share this poem with the world to encourage peace and tranquillity instead of hatred and war.

One day this poem will land in Bosnia again, with a powerful message from fellow citizens of this world urging history to never repeat itself.

By reading this poem you too can become one of her children, and, without ever going to war, keep Bosnia forever free.

Written by: Mirsad Solakovic
Bosnian/English Actor

TABLE OF CONTENTS

FIRST CHAPTER

THE BOY WHO SAID NOTHING
(part I)

Silence is only till the crucial moment,
As when two joints meet,
Which are far from one another
Many long days and years
Many green hills and floral meadows;
Or when, before the decisive battle
In the early dawn, armies merge
Columns fill big valleys
And flags rise decisively towards sky;
Or when it thunders and flashes
And suddenly the hill moves
River cuts a newbed
And changes its course.

It happens in that moment
When there is no more anger in the body,
So it says loudly and clearly why it is suffering and
Wants to respond to injustice with spite.

It happened to me on the judgment day,
When destiny knocked on the door to interrupt my
childhood,
And in one mere moment,

9

The boy grew up,
The boy became a mature man,
The boy was now the guardian of the family.
The boy standing at the edge of an abyss
In front of him wild beasts
Were growling threateningly
While the circle around him was constricting.

"Tell us!
Tell us the secret!"
With a knife in his hand the brute, a monster,
A barbarianis shouting
And threatening to cut the boy's veins.
The parents have lost their breath
They are being shaken by fear
Trauma has become an open wound
Which remains until the Day of Judgment.
The boys tears dried up,
His scream died out,
The sun was extinguished
The whole universe
Disappeared in a black hole in a single moment.

The boy did not say one word
He looked defiantly into the eyes of the beast

While he was being put through infernal torture
Throughout the long days and endless nights.
He had given his father a vow of silence
When he was telling him in the quiet night
That the dogs of war might come to the door
And you need not be scared,
Because their hate cannot harm you.
"My dear son, be happy and live for my sake,
Keep the secret deep inside yourself
and do not tell them under any threat
What you know, for they know not what is in your head.
Do not tell them anything about me.
Just keep quiet -your silence will distract them.
The secret must stay inside you.
My dear son, be happy and live for my sake,
Maybe it means that they threaten to kill you,
But your silence will only distract them.
In your silence you will find the peace,
Which glows eternally as the flame of life.
My son my words might be big or small,
might be worthy or maybe without any hope,
But in the right moment
they will give you support and hope
Which will help you to win the decisive battle.

The boy said nothing,
He did not reveal the secret to the monsters
Even though they engraved on his chest a
Bitter wound with a sharp knife.

Watching his family in shock
Without a word he said
My mother, don't worry!
No, it is not my blood which is flowing
That is their shame flowing
Down my chest
And drawing these beasts to hell
where they shall be eternally tortured!
The joy of the sun is waiting for us
After this gloomy night
Don't worry my dear mother
Just peacefully close your eyes
And wait to be woken by the
Magic song of the birds!

SPLENDOUR OF TRUTH

Everything that we saw,
Heard and knew
we can't see now and we no longer want to know.
What happened - we knew,
but we don't want to know now.

Evil has repeated itself,
and we fear that it will happen again,
but it is all because we fear to tell the truth.

The truth is sometimes harder to tell
than to experience.

Why must one nation go through a path of
suffering, while the rest of the world turns a blind
eye?

MYSTERIOUS RIVER BANKS

History flows through the current of the river
Starenica of Kozarac. Murky and fast
it meanders between mountains of Krajina[1]
through the field where Grmec[2] and Kozara[2] meet
and where it calms down as a ladybird
calms its strong wings and a gurgle of water spills
over the greenery where from time to time birds'
magical singing can be heard.

The meandering river remembers numerous events
that have shaped the course of history.
The clear water remembers the conquerors and
also defenders.

[1]Region in Bosnia and Herzegovina
[2] Mountains in Bosnia and Herzegovina

Murky water remembers
heroes - and also cowards
fast water remembers
horsemen - and also tanks
wise water remembers

firelocks - and also howitzers.

Starenica was waded by commanders
and also by audacious armies.
The river is still healing from its wounds
Inflicted not only by fire and steel, but also by
dead civilians and warriors which it carried.

There are still the old and mysterious water mills
on the river of Kozarac. To witness centuries past
and how once upon a time
The mighty river milled white flour
and fed the people of Krajina.

The banks of Starenica
remember harsh years
at the begining of the nineties.
They remember the dark twentieth century
when exchanges of gunfire were held from both
sides of the river bank.
They remember the exchanges which destroyed the
walls and roofs of
houses and homes, inhabited by both animals and
humans.

Only scorched land remained, ashes and rubble,
covered with corpses which interrupted
Children's games.

The Rika river remembers everything;
it sings epic melodies with waves and waterfalls.
It lures dreamy trekkers into stopping by, even if
just for a moment,to hear her mysterious and
untold stories.
Stories which are hiding beneath demolished walls,
stories which are napping in old stumps, which are
walking in the meadows with a cricket's symphony
which are echoing in waves with sparrows chirping
and pigeons cooing.

Falconers are hiding, and also falcons
with grooms are hiding and also black horses
and that secret chain connects
generations that haven't yet been born.
The truth is a glorious testament of a victory
which prevails even in the darkest of night and
cannot be turned off.
Meandering river remembers
and the memories revive.

SMALL FIRST GRADER

The words are knitted, born and raised
and they rise high to the sky.
They fly, fly day and night
and reach shiny stars.

"Go son!" says the mother
"Recite stanzas and rhymes!
Show that little glow
which dances in your heart!"

On the benches tots are sitting
princes and princesses,
they are waiting for the bell to ring,
so they can go home.

After the first day in school my
heart is beating fast, my soul is singing,
my first grader is hurrying home
to lay in his grandma's lap with a song.

HAPPINESS CANNOT BE STOLEN

Happiness is a secret!
Happiness is a fairy tale!
Happiness is the most beautiful dream.
Happiness is a bird!
Happiness is flight!
Happiness is a new, sunny day.

Happiness flashes, then disappears
without people it has no meaning
it grows like an invisible plant
with mysterious blossoms and scents.

With my head held high I am walking down the
road, searching for a sky full of hope,
the stars are circling around me
this happiness cannot be stolen!

Happiness is hope which blooms in hearts,
grows and changes, like the world itself.
Even if it leaves, a strong wind will bring it back
and it continues to follow my steps.

Happiness is a secret!

Happiness is a fairy tale!
Happiness is the most beautiful dream.
Happiness is a bird!
Happiness is a flight!
Happiness is a new, sunny day.

OLD LOVE

It is that old love
which is never forgotten and never ends ...

I have been holding these two hands for over
seventy years,
which have passed very fast...
like wind through leaves and branches.
These hands were the first to fall into my arms and
enveloped this little bit of soul,
those blue eyes have tricked me
and made me happy forever...

It was that old love by the Mill,
where I found my happiness
and I have stayed there by the Mill forever....

I have stayed with Ramo
in that small village
where nice people
have accepted me and have grown fond of me
as if I were born there with him...

Children were born

there in that community,
in love has widened its rose,
and has set its roots for good
in that small village of mine...

That rose has expanded
and has spread its flowers to fill the village
and to increase its root
and it has beautified its bloom.

Those old hands of mine
with veins like roots
have left memories in my heart
which will never leave me
and which don't know how to betray.

GRANDPA'S GULCH

     In a deep gulch
where a clear stream runs
grandpa's mill rises
from trees and fernery
     in a deep gulch.

There started the peaceful life
of my old grandpa
there today, though he is gone,
all still reminds me of him
     where he started his peaceful life.

Agile hands of the good old man
have arranged grooves carefully
and from a wilderness have created
a captivating small paradise,
     agile hands of the good old man.

Many people were admiring
how he deals with it
and also today - they are admiring
how he raised the small mill,
     Many people were admiring.

And while quiet water is running
he puts some small fish
for Mirso and Meliha
to play in a stream,
        while quiet water is running.

Other kids also come,
So a real hubbub has been made
 tweets of birds are echoing
and there is no end of happiness
        when other kids come.

Many years have passed
my grandpa is around no more,
but the mill is still grinding,
because papa is protecting its beams
        and many years have passed.

SARAJEVO, THE CITY OF MINE

Sarajevo is always in my heart
and it will always be the capital city.
It always gives me a feeling of
youth and splendour, it puts a smile
on my face like a most wanted gift.
There is only one hill above, šeher" [5]
on which Bijela tabija[6]shines.
There is only one Miljacka, fast river,
which meanders between sharp boulders.
There is only one   aromatic Baščaršija[7]
where Sebilj[8], full of pigeons, glows.
There is only one cold river Bosna
Which rises below mount Igman.

I shook hands with CengicVila[9],
Otoka[9], Ilidza[9].
That is my Sarajevo,
which always grows inside me,

───────────

[5] "šeher" is a Turkish word which means „city" but it is still used today to
express love for the city

27

[6] "Bijela tabija" or "White Bastion", old fort overlooking the historic core of Sarajevo
[7] Sarajevo's old bazaar and the historical and cultural centre of the city
[8] The "Sebilj" is an Ottoman-style wooden fountain (sebil) in the centre of Bascarsija

My youthful dreams
revived
when I met happy Sarajevo ladies
who beside Miljacka[10] had flourished
and who bestowed a first kiss upon me
on Wilson promenade
in the shadow of aromatic linden trees...

They say by Bey's Mosque[11]
running white water rises,
who ever drinks that cold water,
he will always return to Sarajevo.
In our hearts we hold your Vječna vatra[12]
which warms us day and night.

---

[9] Sarajevo neighbourhoods (Čengić Vila, Ilidža, Otoka)
[10] River that passes through Sarajevo
[11] Gazi-HusrevBey's Mosque

[12]the Eternal Flame – a memorial to the military and civilian victims of
the Second World War in the centre of Sarajevo

You are gorgeous, Jerusalem of Europe
which glows in Bosnia like a diamond.
Don't give up Sarajevo!
- the good people are depending on you.
We won't let you go!
You belong to Bosnia and Herzegovinia.
We admire you!
- the whole world is sighing.
We love you!
- you are the splendid flower of the Balkans.
Sarajevo you are my city
- you are our mother.
My dearest city
- you are our pride.
Live long for many centuries
for our sake.

Sarajevo, we dream of you
you are our inspiration,
you are our pride
and you have always stood by us.
When our false friends
were hitting us from the hills

we were heroically defending our Sarajevo
while divine Vijecnica[13] was burning.
[13]The City Hall

Women of Sarajevo were walking behind
barricades with their heads high.
They were feeding hungry pigeons
and singing sevdalinke songs[14].
The years of suffering are behind us,
when darkness fell on Bosnian soil.
Today we travel around the world
and bear yellow lilies in our hearts.
My citizens of Sarajevo
are always good men and
they always know, even in their sleep,
who supports, Željo"[15], and who supports
Sarajevo".
Our fans are born,
our mighty BH Fanaticos [16]
who understand the eternal flame
of defiant love
that burns for Bosnia
and feeds our soul!
Sarajevo, you are my favourite city in the world,
I always wear your shirt with pride

[14] traditional genre of folk music
[15] a football club from Sarajevo
[16] the largest supporters' group in Bosnia and Herzegovina who follow Bosnian national sport teams mostly in football, basketball, handball and sitting volleyball

in the East, West,
North and South!
All over the world.
Sarajevo is always in my heart
and it will always be the capital city
that will always give me feelings of
youth and splendour.
It puts a kind smile
on my face, like a most precious gift.

MY DEAR BOSNIANS

Dear Bosnians,
You have always been my biggest strength
and my biggest support,
which leads me toward success
and supports my good deeds.

True support is a power
which is always dear
which gives a zest for life,
fills our souls with a wish
that a man lives for love and freedom.

As a child I started on that small road;
I directed my ideas towards small moments
which have now become exciting big moments.

School is an experience which develops honour
and humanity,
which establishes morals for a developed society.
We always were, and we will always be
on the road which leads to honour.

My favourite moments are there by my house,
on the doorstep where they love me the most.

That is my only land - joyful Bosnia!
My dear proud homeland.

LIFE

Life flows like wild water,
life flourishes like a dense forest,
life carries a laughter as well as bitter tears.
Life gives you all and then it takes it all!

Life goes - rolls happily along,
but happiness doesn't last eternally.
A blizzard buries everything in snow,
shackles streams and rocks with ice.

Life is like a river,
in a moment it is clean and beautiful,
in a moment it is wild and turbid,
in a moment it threatens and
in a moment it sings.

Life is like time
An eternal dance of good and evil.
A game of darkness and light.
In a moment it is dark and in a moment the sun
shines.
Life is like a riddle
which a meandering river

fast and deep
carries through endless time.

SECOND CHAPTER

THE BOY WHO SAID NOTHING
(part II)

Many years have passed.
The boy who said nothing
is walking down the streets of London
while rain is drizzling
he stops by the Thames
and remembers his Kozarac[17].
In the waves of the big river
he hears the gurgle of his Starenica
calling him
to come to the river banks
to reveal the secrets to him,
which it has been keeping for years,
which it has been hiding for decades,
which it has been concealing for centuries,
because nobody understands
its songs, its rhymes
and they don't hear the voice
which tells us the stories.

---

[17]a town in north-western Bosnia and Herzegovina

Many years later,
the boy who kept the secret
that was hiding in his heart,

a secret was revealed.
It was levitating in the Universe
and made him realise that there are
men and non-men that exist in the world.
Some have souls and others don't.
Love opens horizons
and hate blinds,
there is no happiness in the misery of others
and that sometimes man is deceived by his own
eyes,
because beneath the skin of lambs wolves are
hiding,
and in that moment a boy becomes a man,
and from the Thames, Kozarac can speak.

FRIENDSHIP
(Dedicated to my namesake Mirso)

There is something in Kozarac
there is something in Sana[18]
there is something in Krajina
        in Bosnia and Herzegovina.

There is something in Birmingham
there is something in London
there is something on the island
        in the United Kingdom.

What gives me the strength
is the friendship from childhood
which lasts despite everything,
        that is the greatest wealth.

There is something on the big screen.
There is something in silver and gold.
There is something in a glittering city;
it might be a briliant success or terrible failure.

_____
[18] a river in the north-western part of Bosnia and Herzegovina

There is something in a long journey
There is something in a great flight

There is something in the passing of time
there is something beneath a burden.

But, friendship that lasts
gives me the new strength
to live, to smile
        to admire the world.

KOZARAC – THE PRETTIEST SMALL TOWN IN THE WORLD

My Kozarac - is my pride!
Joy for our souls -for our hearts!
A source of happiness - for my homeland!
        -My Kozarac - is my pride!

My dear people of Kozarac
they are sweet and kind
and they always wish well for everyone
        -My dear people of Kozarac.

They always carry their town in their hearts
wherever they stand, wherever they walk
wherever they fly, wherever they sail
        -they carry their town in their thoughts and
hearts.

They remember their youth
like captivating blossom and ripe fruit
welcoming eyes and warm smiles
        -they remember their dear youth.

*

In a small, but big town

in Kozarac my mother gave birth to me,
my mother gave birth to a fierce man from Krajina
        - in a small, but big town.

As soon as I could stand on my feet,
I was running far through meadows, the
stars were calling me as soon as I got up on my
feet.

*

Hate struck Kozarac
suddenly - unprovoked by anything
people are led to death camps
        -hate struck Kozarac.

Hate struck Kozarac,
The war, akin to a tsunami, destroyed everything
not a single brick was left
        -hate struck Kozarac.

The hate that blinds reason
descended on the streets of Kozarac
and struck down both grandson and old man
        -the hate that blinds reason.

The hate that blinds reason

was brought by ghostly dogs of war
they pushed Kozarac through the doors of hell
        - the hate that blinds reason.

What must never be forgotten
is the painful look of the man from Manjaca[19]
with his ribs protruding through his skin, he was
the camp prisoner of Omarska[19]
        -it must never be forgotten.

What must never be forgotten
is the barbed wire around Keraterm[19],
Trnopolje[19] and Tomasica[20] camps
cruel shooting of the innocents
on the rocks of Koricani
        -it must never be forgotten.

Remembrance is a Bosnian testament
Remembering missing persons
who are being searched for by relatives
whose souls are still without peace
        -remembrance is a Bosnian testament.

---

[19]concentration camp
[20] mass grave Koricanske stijene

*

In a remote world a desire is burning,
the expelled returned to their birth place
to build again paradise in it
        -in a remote world a desire is burning.

They built our Kozarac from scratch
in their soul they have the vow of peace
hard working hands astonished the whole world
        -they built our Kozarac from scratch.

Full of optimism and love
people of Kozarac are dreaming while touring the
planet, dreaming
of the prettiest little town in the world
        - full of optimism and love.

Mesmerizing glitz of Hollywood
Adorns Kozarac in everyone's dream
in summer or cold winter
        -mesmerizing glitz of Hollywood.

*

The old tower of Kozarac remains, built from
mighty walls, it has stood by the road since ancient
times
        -the old tower of Kozarac.

It witnessed ancient times and
reminds us of glorious battles
captains and daring rebels
        -it witnessed ancient times.

Cannons were striking with fire
from the fortified tower of Krajina
when empires clashed
        -cannons were striking with fire.

Black horses were rushing
into the distance across the fields whilst
heroic hearts were rising up to the heights
        -while black horses were rushing.

To be raised from the ground
that is the destiny of Kozarac
whenever a new age comes
        -to be raised from the ground.

The tower of Kozarac remembers well

who Omer-pasha Latas was
and how a bad reputation followed him
        -the tower of Kozarac remembers well.

It remembers also May of '92
when it was besieged by the beasts
who were seeking reasons for crime in their
religion
        -it remembers also May of '92.

But hate did not defeat love, even though
innocent people perished,
because the people of Kozarac are survivors.
        -but hate didn't defeat love.

                    * *

We remember coffin to coffin
we remember grave stone to gravestone
we remember, so it cannot be forgotten
        - so evil will never be repeated.

We remember death camps
        we remember barbed wire,
we remember children and fathers
        we remember necks cut,

we remember mutilated faces
      we remember murderers' laughter,
we remember guards of death
      we remember walls of blood,
we remember the torture of the innocents
      we remember piles of shot people,
we remember mass graves
      we remember court rooms of The
Hague,
we remember genocide deniers
      we remember big mouths without shame,
      we remember names in stone
      we remember crime in time.

We remember coffin to coffin
we remember gravestone to gravestone
we remember so it can not be forgotten
      - so evil will never repeat itself.

CHAMPION
(Dedicated to Fikret Hodzic)

Always cheerful, beloved by everyone
a champion - our Fikro!
Full of life, smiling,
An adorable person.
Fifteen-time winner of Mr Yugoslavia
year to year representing his country
on the winning pedestal
a super champion - our Fikro!

From childhood he loved
bodybuilding and with home made weights
he trained the whole day,
the gym was a magnet to him.
Halima, his hard working mother
had no idea back then that she had given birth to a
legend.
An inspirationwho shall be admired by many.
Fikro was going to be a champion
who would be remembered by the world.
Fikro would come to make a friend by the name of
Arnold Schwarzenegger.
But when the Krajina fell into darkness
and when the world remained without hope
and when flowers remained without scent

and smiles of happiness froze
in the summer of '92
the sun darkened by grief
then the dogs of war began to bark,
qualm fell on a simple folk.
Hell fire spoke out
innocent people died because of hate.
Krajina men were being persecuted by beasts
led to death camps
they found reasons, because of their religion,
to torture innocent people.

Thus they came to our champion,
evil souls in human form
they deprived him of life on his doorstep
and threw accolades and medals on the fire.

But it is not possible to kill the glow in a heart.
Death isn't the end of a legend.
Krajina, Bosnia and the World are still being
warmed by Fikro, the champion - who smiles.

WORDS OF A HERO
(Dedicated to Osman Solakovic)

In a defiant Bosnia, in the bitter Krajina,
the hero and the flower are speaking
Osman is talking with the lily
beside the Sana river- where the meadow is green
and the hero's words are echoing
through days and years
through living memory.

Osman is a symbol of our majesty,
our past, present and future.
The beat of his brave heart empowers us and
comfort us in our dreams.
He gave us a crucial grain of hope
to stay there - on our own
and defend our pride,
our majesty...

My Osman,
we don't have you any more,
but this verse will always warm us
and will open new horizons to us.
You were that firm stone of ours
that didn't want to give up Bosnia,

for our bitter Krajina
you didn't leave even a shred of hope to your
enemy
that is our man from Krajina.

Osman's message goes on, he never surrenders,
his streng this his heart beat
which binds us and makes us all stronger.

Through time
the words of our Osman echo:
"People, don't give up what is ours!
Have hope in the barricades of Kozarac
that are going to defend our doorsteps!
Foes are dreaming to take them from us,
our children and our mothers
the justice is only in the hands
of one hero!
Don't give up Bosnia for my sake!
Don't give up our homeland for my sake!"
I'm lying there - in a meadow in Krajina
upon which golden lilies
bloom.

Osman's words echo
and emerald Una [21] carries them down Krajina

and they echo through Bosnia
through days and years
like a sun of hope
like a message of wisdom
and like a warning:
for the dead
and for the living
and for those - not yet born:
bitter people from Krajina
and proud
Bosnians and Herzegovinians!

---

[21] river in Croatia and Bosnia and Herzegovina

UNCLE

My uncle left with his head turned
away
from his doorstep.
He parted from his wife and children
and the most beloved little pet
the cuddly puppy
who had always been beside him.

Sorrow has remained, misery has remained,
no one has ever found a single trace.
Only the last words
of my uncle have remained:
"My children, this is no good,
they are plotting against our lives in secret.
Give me a glass of water
to clear my soul
which the enemy has not taken away yet."

He emptied the glass of cold water
and left down the curved path
to eternal tranquillity.

GRANDPA

We had something
that no one before us had.
We loved someone
Who some never had the honour of meeting.
Our grandpa - Ramo Solak!
He always stood firm with us;
in good times or bad.
We always knew who would be the first to support
our wishes.

Our pride is always with us,
one that started with him
and was directed by him
and let it be recorded that:
Our grandpa - Ramo Solak
Will stand by us
forever!

Grandpa, we are always with you till the end
and you are with us too,
regardless of the condition you are in.
You are our beginning,
our tough foundation
which is embedded in our hearts,

you are our pride, our roots
hero to our families
forever.

HERO NIJAZ - BOSNIAN DRAGON

Kozarac heedfully keeps memories
Of fierce and courageous fighters
Nijaz is a scent - which captivatingly lasts
Nijaz iz the golden lily - of Kozarac.

He left everything he had
with sadness, he left his warm home and
gave everything for the homeland.
He was defending freedom and liberty.

The hero is going home
with a heavy foreboding in his heart:
"Wait, dad - I'm close by
once again I long to see your eyes!"

But his dad left without farewell,
so his wish remained unfulfilled
with a gun in his hand he went to fight in the
trenches.
He became a living target when the battle started.

Nijaz defended his land with his comrades.
He gave hope and safety to his people.

He manned front lines throughout his homeland.
In Nijaz's heart - there lies a true Bosnian dragon.

"Let's go foward - assault!"
-Golden lilies are going to attack
to liberate a beloved homeland
from our enemies.

That shameful aggressor
is strong while attacking unarmed civilians
while torturing the weak in concentration camps.
But when ghazis enter the battlefield
suddenly they don't want to fight.
They run away–they leave their weapons.
We took back our beloved Bosnia.

The golden lily fell in battle
while he was attacking bravely
to accomplish his great dream
to make Kozarac free again.

UNTIL THE DAY OF JUDGMENT
(Dedicated to Muharem Balic)

Muharem kissed two grandsons
And left
as if he exited a fairy tale...

with a golden smile
Those were the last kisses
for his tots
who were making him happy.

He is gone too young
on the road without return
neither guilty nor responsible.

He moved to a better place,
to eternal ahiret[22].
It is not possible to forgive
heartless villains
who shortened his life
and separated him from us.

His daughter prays for him every night

and whispers words which come from the heart:

"That love, pride and warmth
I am going to give to my sons,
so they remember their grandfather,
my father
and carry him in their heart
until the Day of Judgment."

Muharem left
as if he exited a fairy tale...

---

[22] Turkish word meaning "heaven"

TOMASICA[20]- NEVER AGAIN

The earth swore to the sky
that nothing inside it
will stay hidden
and will sooner or later be revealed.

The wind rose and started to blow.
Dogs, wolves and sheep wonder
What moans drearily?
On a hill which is called Tomasica[20]
in a small grove
a forest moans and branches shake
leaves fall to emphasize the sorrow.

A landowner watches his land,
listens to the painful and sad voices
that are creepily echoing down the meadow
until the early dawn...

The earth cries
the innocent buried bodies cry,
but locals live there normally
without realizing the extent
of unseen atrocities.

Lifeless skeletons are lying all around
they will not leave the place
until human souls find
eternal tranquillity
in the grave,
in the graveyard
not thrown in a pit,
a shameful mass grave
where skeletons are intermingled
where bones are mixed
where skulls are shattered.

Terrible crimes happened so quickly
so quietly,
that no one could even think
how much evil
is hidden beneath that fatal hill.

Tomasica - torment of Bosnia
Europe and World!
Tomasica - your name
shall be written with black ink
in memory of civilisation
and a river of tears cannot wash away
the pain which bears your name

Tomasica - abyss of torment!

On a barren lea,
not even donkeys graze there, nor horses
nor cows nor sheep
not even one tree grows there anymore.

What was there?
What happened there?
Why are those leas and hills eerily deserted?
What kind of a disaster came upon that place,
that neither grass nor snow will cover it now.
There is no tranquillity for animals or for
people,until the secret that hides beneath the
bosom of tragic Tomasica is revealed
from that spacious black hollow
where cries died and horror froze.

The old villager spoke out;
he could not take that horror with him to the grave
the hole is too small
the coffin is too narrow to contain all that torment
and horror.

The earth opens beneath the sky

A Mass grave opens
vainly hidden terrible truths
are revealed
to remind us
not to forget
so Bosnia and Herzegovina remembers
and Europe remembers
and the civilized World remembers
that horrible crime wrought upon innocent people.
Never must it be repeated:
Tomasica- never again!

THIRD CHAPTER

THE BOY WHO SAID NOTHING
(part III)

The silence lasted many long days and years, until
the crucial moment; when two sparks were
reunited and then ignited.

Here tonight memories are stirring.
All the hopes and suffering in my chest have
stopped.
I have been carrying them for two decades
the secret will reveal itself to the World
through yearning songs,
through quiet rhymes
and I shall give a name for every sorrow.
Let it be a reminder
to all well-wishing people.

LAST LOOK

(Dedicated to Mirsad Hodzic who was thrown off The Rocks of Koricani)

Hordes of evil separated two brothers
One left, one right,
"My dear brother, we are not together anymore."

They separated two hearts with guns
They separated two souls with wire.
Sorrow surrounded both of them
We looked at eachother:
      Tears are coming, my heart is pounding
      my lungs are tense
      as if it was my last breath.

The soul was sobbing internally
not releasing a sound
searching for the friendly hand
which will bring salvation:
"Don't take my brother away from me!
I only have him as my pride!"

The foes took the young souls,
but that still was not their end
a little bit of hope remained in me
that destiny will reunite them.

75

The Rocks of Koricani were glaring in the sun
on that fatal August of ninety-two
when columns of buses
stopped by the cursed abyss.
The abyss gapes before the feet
of forcefully transported civilians.
While armed dogs of war
are watching them with bestial eyes.

Young souls were in distress
their eyes tricked them
above the bottomless abyss.
One by one - they are falling
the end came to them all,
the people are swallowed by the abyss
without a trace.

The bodies fly like swallows through the sky
Their cries echoed down into the depths as they
disappeared, like fading lights they were
extinguished, their souls extinguished
the soul went to the point of no return.
"So my dear brother Mica also
found there the splendour of Jannah[23]."

---

[23] an eternal place for Muslim people

76

SUPPORT
(For friend Kemo)

The deep words
from the bottom of my soul
wake dispersed silences
unlock wounded souls
and give their miraculous power.

"Keep what is yours and take care of yourself
and never fall in despair."

Things will come and things will go,
but good relationships will stay between good
people.
They will always live and
they will awake them at the right time
and catch them in bad moments
and paint them in joyful colours.

OLD MOSTAR BRIDGE

Old Bridge,
nobody has ever managed to erase its arch.
The tumultuous centuries flew across it,
the greatest military leaders from the whole World
and they have carried across countless treasures
and piles of weapons
Old Bridge is our dearest rose.

That is our pride,
our scented rose
which connects Bosnia with Herzegovina.
They are two wings of our country
that could never run from each other.
That Old Bridge of ours binds them
connects us, strengthens us and never betrays us.

That Old Bridge awakes us in the night
to keep the old love secrets
which were born and flourished there
like young snow flakes
down by the bank of river Neretva.

Love is born again on the Old Bridge

Its strengthens its weakly wings
prepares it for magical flight,
for departure into the distance
to a far away World
across its hills and high mountains,
carrying inside the heart a secret
which the white Old Bridge keeps
in Neretva.

They all have become part of that bridge
they all have become part of that love
and they never have enough of it.
They all used to dive from the old bridge
and became heroes of that city
from there Mirsad, dubbed Mica jumped and the
legend of the Old Bridge was born.

Everyone knows who the old Mica was
and how many times he jumped from the old
bridge
and how many trophies he won
and how he entertained young ladies
and how he built his youth with the old bridge...

Books are written about those men with brave
hearts.

The jumpers who were flying through the sky like
swallows
and jumping to Neretva's embrace
that beautiful green clear water.

The Old Bridge remembers well,
military leaders and heroes
walking upon it
leaving legends behind them.

Separated banks of Neretva hurt
where the white arch once stood hurts
it has been glittering for centuries
on it young bridge keepers were walking,
guardians of the bridge,
after whom the city got its name

      Mostar[24]!

After ten long years
once again the glamorous bridge
emerged from the green water
and a gorgeous white arch
shone above Neretva
like a dream vision
it reunited separated banks

it reunited east with west.

---

[24] from the Bosnian word „most" which means „bridge".

LOVE

Love is a beauty that we admire!
Why are we sometimes ashamed of it?
when we know it rules inside us
and opens hidden doors of emotion and power?

It smiles sometimes to everybody
and it affects people differently.
Someone covers his eyes
someone's cheeks blush
but blood rushes
through everybody's veins equally.

Love is youth
love is maturity
love is a secret
that man cannot divulge.

Love is a monument which glows from within
which nobody can steal
it is always there to remind us
of days full of hope:
"Love is a pleasant dream that can suprise us all,
like a rainy day in a spring."

Love is like a box
Sometimes it is empty, and sometimes it is full of
hope,
but it is always there inside you
all the time
from the beginning and remaining till the end.

SREBRENICA – 8372...

Srebrenica - My incomprehensible grief...

Eight thousand three hundred and seventy-two
Violently extinguished human lives
horrible genocide
executing civilians
executing kids and old men
executing men and women
executing innocent people
because of their faith
because of their names
because of their surnames
because of something which is not their own
choice,
but which destiny determined for them.

Eight thousand three hundred and seventy-two
- lapidary inscriptions in Potocari
where white gravestones are standing
side by side
mute witnesses of a crime
a reminder to the people
to the Balkans, to Europe and to the World

about our civilisation and of mankind.
Eight thousand three hundred and seventy-two sad
stories
of which we know only some
and because of which our blood freezes in our
veins.
Sad tear of Srebrenica,
you have dropped on the soul of the World
and touched many human hearts.
After twenty years
the search still remains
for the perished innocent victims
of monstrous genocide
and for the butchers of my people.
There is no refuge, either in a dream or in reality,
because there is no oblivion:
Man, do not forget Srebrenica,
so evil will never repeat itself
Not ever and to nobody.
Man, don't forget Ramo
who was forced by the villains
to call his son Nermin to death!
Ramo and also Nermin were cruelly killed.

But why?
What did they do wrong?

Echos of the eery voices resonate through
Srebrenica
through the Balkans, through Europe and through
the World
and they will resonate until the Day of Judgment
as a reminder to all people.

Oh, my World
where is your conscience and where is your soul?
Don't you remember
that justice is implacable.

Srebrenica - My incomprehensible grief...

SUCCESS OF OUR PEOPLE

We must support
our successful people around the World,
we must exaggerate their good deeds,
protect good people
because fairness and honour are always hard to
earn.

These are the people our country Bosnia needs
for whom it always yearns.

Wake up Bosnians
and support our hopes,
liberate our hearts
from hate, grief and misery
and fill yourself with warmth,
love, happiness and joy.

Invest effort and knowledge into good deeds
and distance yourselves from evil and treachery.

Don't believe in those people
who don't wish good to other people,
love and respect others

boast about the success
of our hardworking people
around the globe.

Poetry, knowledge, sport
Connect noble people
represent your homeland
expand your homeland
and magnify your people
one Nation
Bosnians around the Globe.

Our people live all over the World
and they are leaving marvelous landmarks behind
them.
We should make a dead knot for the evil and the
hate
and bind our hearts with warmth and love.

THANK YOU, HOMELAND

With safe steps I walk
I carry my homeland in my heart
The love inside me is stronger
than all the challenges of life.

Thank you my father!
Thank you my mother!
Thank you my my grandfather!
Thank you my grandmother!

I am grateful to you, Krajina!
I am grateful to you, Bosnia and Herzegovina!
Because in my heart there is no
place for hate.

CHILDREN

Children are the future
Children are the peace
Children are the harmony
Children will destroy the wall of hate.

Children are the wings of hope
Children are the smile of happiness
Children are the shiny stars
Children are the most beautiful flowers.

Love life
love people
Hear children's voices:
"In love is the salvation
for the whole World - for us all!"

Live together with one another
respect the freedom of others
build your home
and feed the white dove of peace.

THE BOY WHO SAID NOTHING
(part IV)

The boy who said nothing
testified with silence:
about the end and the beginning
about the nonsense and the sense
about the day and the night
about the fear and the power
about the man and the no-man
about the life and the death
about the love and the hate
about the light and the fire
about the hope and the suffering
about the last person and the first person
about the dead person and the living person.
and when he spoke out:
- A CHANT ECHOED-
A hymn to the man with his head held high
witness of truth for all times.

EPITAPH

Kind words will always fill our hearts with love.
Humans feed their souls with nice feelings.
Love connects people and makes them happy.
Human reason frees human conscience from bad
contemplations.

Human behaviour adorns his look
and finds good people.
Human contact can be a good opportunity or bad
opportunity,
So take up the challenge and establish
conversation.
Those people who know how to appreciate and
respect themselves,
will always appreciate and respect others too.
Mercy is born, happiness is found, and kindness is
achieved.

AUTHOR BIOGRAPHY

Mirsad Solaković was born in 1978 in Kozarac, Bosnia and Herzegovina. He finished seventh grade at the Secondary school "BratstvoTrnopolje". At the begining of the war in 1992 he escaped to England with his immediate family: father - Mehmed Solakovic, mother - Zumra Solakovic, sister - Meliha Solakovic, brother - Jasmin Solakovic.

Mirsad continued secondary school and successfully enrolled in Sixth form College studying A level Drama. Subsequently he gained a BA (HONS) in Theatre Studies and Professional Practice from Coventry University, which allowed him to further study drama at the Birmingham School of Acting; obtaining a Masters degree in Acting. Following this he gained a teaching qualification at Wolverhampton University. During this time, he wrote short plays, monologues and poetry. In addition, he was also working as an actor working both in the UK and internationally.

His writing includes various short scripts for Theatre in Education companies. One such work is, "The Victims Of War".This was based on his childhood experiences in Bosnia and Herzegovina, and was an attempt to dramatise the experiences of children in Bosnia during the war. Written in English, it sought to communicate this experience to a UK audience. He adapted a previously written personal journal, outlining the main chronological events of the war for the British stage; this was given the title "Diary of Events". It was performed at the Birmingham Repertory Theatre, and later throughout England.

By the age of fourteen he filmed his first documentary "From Bosnia and Back", which featured him and his family, and was broadcast on local television. In 2005 he made a documentary with BBC producer, Howard Perks called: "The Young Successful East European People", broadcast both in the UK and the Balkans.

He was one of the principle characters in a large scale, sight specific community theatre project called: "UN-EARTH". This involved 250 actors and musicians on various stages and locations, requiring the audience to move around and experience the action over two hours at numerous settings and installations. It was recorded on DVD and distributed throughout the UK.

Mirsad subsequently collaborated with the highly regarded UK playwright and academic Peter Cann, in order to co write a screenplay about his experiences during the war.

As a result of this prolific work rate, further acting opportunities materialised in the form of more stage and TV appearances both in the UK and in Bosnia. He was invited as a guest on various shows back in his homeland. He appeared in a film by Jasmin Durakovic called: "Ja sam iz Krajine, zemlje kestena" ("I'm from Krajina, The Land of The Chestnut"), starring as Mujo Hrnjica.

His career has more recently been focused on his Bosnian community in Birmingham, centred around the Bosnian UK

Network. Here he often participates in various events and programmes; he has written and performed various plays there focusing on the Bosnian war. He is actively engaged in voluntary work, and in his free time he works with children, and uses acting as a therapy for mental and physical illness. He has also generated humanitarian initiatives, organising convoys to his homeland during the recent floods.

* * *

Mirsad appeared in the touring theatre piece "The Boy Who Said Nothing". Written by Greg Hobbs, who together with Mirsad formed "GREGOMIR" Theatre company, which has performed across the UK and in Bosnia. The current plan is to carry this forward and present this play to as wide an audience as possible. So far the reaction from both UK and Bosnian audiences has been universally positive, and this has been from a variety of age groups and has regularly been described as "inspiring".

Mirsad, is regularly called upon as a motivational speaker, and relates his own journey and experiences in the context of being an architect for change and for overcoming difficulties and challenges, particularly those relating to young people. He is able to relate how own traumatic experiences impacted on his early life, and how his positive attitude has brought him to where he is today.

One of Mirsad's goals is, to encourage a free exchange of experiences and mutual understanding between British and

103

Bosnian theatre, to build a metaphoric bridge between the two nations, just like the bridge at Mostar, an eternal link between two communities. To learn from each other in the spirit of mutal respect.

In the future, it is Mirsad's goal to secure funding to produce a film by adapting the already established and well received theatre script "The Boy Who Said Nothing". This anthology of poems will help to make that dream a reality. There is then a sense that this story, the story of Mirsad's journey has not yet been completely told. He races towards it's next chapter with hope, enthusiasm and expectation.

Review of the text; "The Boy Who Said Nothing", author Mirsad Solakovic:

VISION OF A BETTER WORLD EXPRESSED THROUGH THE LANGUAGE OF ART

I) General notes about the project and the book

The book of poetry by Mirsad Solakovic, entitled "The Boy Who Said Nothing" is an authentic experience of the Bosnian and Herzegovinian tragedy. It was caused by multiple aggressions against the Republic of Bosnia and Herzegovina in the period 1992-1995, which was marked by horrifying crimes inflicted upon the civilian population, qualifed by numerous judicial sentences as a genocide, and verified by numerous relevant political decisions around the world.

Besides the great number of poetry works which testify about the golgotha of Bosnia and Herzegovina, and mostly Bosniaks, during the last war, Solakovic's work is specific, because it does not bind thematically to any one part of the country. Instead it describes the crimes which occurred across our homeland.

He talks about the destuction and celebrates the reconstrucion of the Old Bridge (Stari most) in Mostar - the cultural symbol of civilsation, the construction that never fails to amaze with its exotic beauty new generations of fans of World Cultural Heritage. The New-Old Bridge is testifying today to the whole world that civilisation was being defended and was defended on the banks of beautiful Neretva, which after the war got a chance to experience its renaissance. It continues to emit messages of peace and love between people, being the bridge between different cultures and civilisations - which is connecting not separating. By rebuilding the Old Bridge, connecting the violently-separated banks of Neretva, it is proved once more that MAN is capable of recognizing and defeating EVIL-which is the obvious threat to truth, justice and freedom - the pillars of humane society.

Audicious Bosnian man, by defending his homeland and the honour of his family, of his village, town and fatherland - he defended his door step wherever he could, and thus he stopped the invasion of evil, which was growing into a global threat to World peace. With great sacrifices, the universal human and cultural values are defended, once again, in these lands. This honourable fight with humane tendencies gave birth to an antifascist conscience, which is in time of peace manifested through preserving the memory of people - who were participants in the war events - who testify about the dreadful crimes and noble heroes who stood up against the invasion of the evil. Patriots of Bosnia and Herzegovina realized that, if suffering and crimes are forgotten, the evil will repeat. Therefore, in peace NEW HEROES are assigned, who, by speaking about the last war and testifying the truth, open the gates of good and open the paths of peace and prosperity in the Balkans.

Artist and humanist Mirsad Solakovic is committed to this honourable and noble path, through sacrifice for the universal good for all the people in the Balkans, as well as in the World. With his multimedia project 'The Boy Who Said Nothing', on which he has been working and with which he has been publicly active for many years, Solakovic gives his contibution, together with his co-workers, so that we can live and work in a better World, in which there will be no violence against people, but life in mutual understanding, solidarity and harmony.

II) Structure of literary work

This conceptual collection of poems "The Boy Who Said Nothing" comprises three chapters, where songs and poems of various thematical and expressional spectrum are classified - from the deep impressions of a boy whose childhood is shortened by the whirlwind of war, over evocations of memories of certain people and authentic events which cut deeply into the consciousness, to descriptions of mass execution sites for civilians, where the gates of hell open. Beside the harsh reality of the war which is often the focus of poetical notations,and where mass and individual anguish is being described, this book abounds with inspired positivism which presents to the reader a VISION OF A BETTER WORLD, expressed with the language of art and composed of words of hope. The author remembers the criminal torture against the the young boy, but at the same time he evokes the strength of the young spirit which defies torments and non-humans; he describes the throwing of innocent civilans from Rocks of Koricani into the abyss, but also a gentle dream of the noble grandpa who in an abandoned gulch builds an astonishing World of harmony; elegant verses talk about the mass slaughtering of innocent people in

Srebrenica and about the horrifying mass grave of "Tomasica", but the Poet's soul is also filled with a juvenile sincere emotion which sees the glow of love that fills noble hearts.

Thematical and content contrasts are one of the basic characteristics of Mirsad Solakovic'spoetical work where readers often find unexpected suprises - given that poetical creation encompasses temporal and spatial mutlidimensionality - breadth and depth - which reaches far into the distant past, navigating through the time machine of the collective memory, all the way to the walks by clear rivers, leafy mountain ranges of natural ambience and urban environments filled with historical secrets. The entire poetical work is conceived to bear suggestive message of love and peace between people of different views and affinities. Despite the dark side of history in which we have immense atrocities and unsanctioned crimes, human hope and faith in people are intensely present which from poem to poem stretch planetary alongside other states and continents, and stay to levitate and radiate positivism in the arms of eternity.

The concept of the book "The Boy Who Said Nothing" has a mosaic character, so every poem can be viewed from at least three aspects: in the context of the entire work (1) - where we find related themes and conceptual entities; in the context of chapters (2) - where three parts are encompassed according to the primarily inner, contents character and thematical differentiation; and function of a poem in itself, as an independent and separate poetical entity (3) - where we can recognize basic aesthetical and literary-craft values.

III) Poetical expression

a) Form and content

The poetry of Mirsad Solakovic in his work: "The Boy Who Said Nothing" is composed in the form of songs and short poems, which is adapted to thematical frameworks and dramaturgical need for elaborating and performing the plot to make the point in an adequate way.

- Poems where the rhythm of stanzas dominates are distinguished by thematical focus, where in the fore front we have the main character or one event with messages that reflect the essence of human character or where we have illuminaton of significant dimensions of the chosen event. These poems are concise, with a harmonious, soft rhythm, and the following poems are classified into this group:: "Grandpa's Gulch ", "Happiness Cannot Be Stolen", 'Small First Grader" etc.

- Poems with a wide spectrum of themes, which can be enclosed with a philosophical thought or a symbolic expression, are significantly present in this collection, and through them the author's deep meaningfulness and affinity towards meditative themes from the sphere of universality and cosmopolitanism are manifested; among them are the poems: "Life", "Love", Friendship" etc.

- The author recites his poems with captivating emotions toward his people and homeland, so patriotism is one of the dominants that strongly determinesthe character of Mirsad Solakovic's poetry , thus making him a recognizably

Bosnian poet, with every verse overflowing with melodious words of love and sincere commitment to his homeland Bosnia and Herzegovina. It is about spiritual connection which means life, the best witness is the intensity of emotional charge in his poems, which does not abate from the beginning to the end of the book. The following poems, among others, are considered to belong into this group: "Thank You, Homeland", "Success of Our People" and "My Dear Bosnians".

   - Poems which describe immediate family, relatives and friends have a special emotional character, where human destinies intermingle in unpredictable and dramatic life paths. A sincere and dedicated relationship with the homeland Bosnia and Herzegovina comes into focus - where patriotism and humanism overlap – the two basic ethical pillars on which all of Mirsad Solakovic's poetry stands. In these poems with specific emotional charge the essence of the literary creation of Bosnia and Herzegovina is expressed in the best way and the human dimension overwhelms as the key dominant and humanism as the fundamental feature of the Bosnian soul expressed via literary-artistic creation. What is obvious in Mirsad Solakovic's poetry and what is the base of the poetry of Bosnia and Herzegovina, is that the spirit of Bosnia lives and survives by living through poetry, which is not only the art, but at the same time the form and the content of spiritual existence, in which we are being convinced by poems like: „Hero Nijaz - The Bosnian Dragon", "Until the Day of Judgment", "Uncle", "Grandpa", "Words of Hero" etc.

Mirsad's poetry, sometimes of a smaller, sometimes of a greater volume, are the most brilliant segment of the entire work. They deal mainly with the inexhaustible theme of crime against the innocent; the crimes of heavily armed beasts against innocent civilians who did not want the war, but who had it forced upon them by an unjust aggression. Poems speak about violently occupied cities, about urbicide and genocide - which is a shameful act of civilisation a product of a deviant ideology - which in the most brutal way deals with the one or the other, but not leaving the possibility of free choice. Different cities and places of Bosnia and Herzegovina - Sarajevo, Mostar, Srebrenica, Kozarac and Tomasica- are sad symbols of torture and suffering of people, who were deprived of freedom of movement and were exposed to torture and agony and to various brutal executions by fascist hordes only because of their name and their faith.

Considering that the horror of crimes exceeds the power of words to authentically describe in human acts against man, and due to the intensity of the crime a man is usually speechless and finds it hard to shape the present pain and sorrow in an artistic manner. Therefore, the success of Mirsad Solakovic is greater and more important, considering the fact that, although there are a great number of books dealing with war suffering in Bosnia and Herzegovina, books where atrocities from the whole of Bosnia and Herzegovina are described are, actually, very rare. Into this group of shorter poems belong: "Sarajevo the City of Mine", "Tomasica- Never Again", Old Bridge",,,Srebrenica – 8372 ...".

111

The poem "The Boy Who Said Nothing" consists of four parts which are placed in all three chapters of the book. It is the main pillar of the entire book, it has 153 verses, and with it the book starts and ends. The boy under the vow of silence endures the enemies' torture in order to protect his family, his most loved ones - father, mother, brother and sister, experiencing distressing drama - realizing that his childhood ended in one moment and that he suddenly grew up. Under the weight of responsibility that has crushed upon his young shoulders, he has not given up, he has stayed on his feet, stayed upright, stayed proud - and the darkness that was threateningly crushing him, encouraged the birth of the light in his soul and his body. This transformation from a boy to a mature person, from hopelessness to hope, from darkness to light, and from silence to words - births the POEM, which carries the message of power and strength, of love and freedom, of truth and justice. Due to the impressive symbolism in the experience and the magnetic universality in the message, the poem "The Boy Who Said Nothing" has a potential to justify the title of the book and deep reasons for a transformation of the message into a general artistic-creative project with film as a final outcome.

b) Expression

The author uses literary-artistic expressional language adapted to the function of form and content of the poem. Therefore, in harmony with thematical compactness, defined professional norms are applied in accordance with aesthetic demands. Thus, the manner which the poet uses to form verses is also variable, so we can notice poems with melodious rhymes, where the rhythm of the verses is a dominant characteristic of professional formation, while in other places we find free-verse poems, where the poem follows the inner rhythm, where even one word, usually a word of a wider context or emphasized by dramaturgical constellation, can have the function of a verse.

1) Expression in the form of a rhyme, and where the rhythm of a verse is also harmonized, is found in the poem " Happiness Cannot Be Stolen":

> „Happiness is hope which blooms
> in the heart
> grows and changes, like the World.
> Even if it leaves - amstrong wind will bring it back
> and it continues to follow my steps."

Besides the contextual broadness encompassed in some verses, concise expression which specifies the meaning is also recognizable, so the uniqueness is present, which gives a stamp of intimate experience to the full meaning of the stanza.

2) We find an example of a formation by using free verses, when every verse is a full picture in the function of purpose, which has a complex and broad spectrum of meaning, in the poem "The Boy Who Said Nothing - I part":

Tear dried up
Scream died out
Sun went out
The whole universe
disappeared in black hole
in only one moment.

But boy did not utter a single word
he looked defiantly into the eyes of the beast
while he was been put through infernal torture
throughout long days and endless nights.

Fragments from the poem describe dramatic events related to the boy who shows courage by defying danger that hovers upon him while responding to torture with categorical silence. The situation in which the boy finds himself is the scene which he carries with him for his whole life. There is no way to erase it from memory, because then the CHANGE that determines future happens. So if, within a man, the dark forces do not overcome - unpleasant events become inexhaustible sources of positive inspiration, which is one of a series of messages of this poetical work, expressed, in greater part, with the language of symbolism.

IV) Conceptual art

Mirsad Solakovic writes equally about the World that he remembers and about the World that he sees. He writes about

114

realism, and also about surrealism, and in his verses both concrete objects and abstract relations are present. Therefore, we can classify Mirsad's poetry under CONCEPTUALISM, because the poetical creation of the poems is in the function of more sublime ideas that reach beyond art and aesthetics, and enter into the sphere of applied arts and obtain social contours. A determinant of poetical engagement is apparent, which though conceptual art has effects in the social sphere - whereby a path is opened for the artist to communicate directly to the audience which feels and follows the public pulse of artistic creation. The specificity of Mirsad Solakovic's poetic expression is also reflected in his gravitation towards the visual, and in the reduction of complex spritual relations to concrete symbols, which reduces his poetry, although complex in content, to a simple expression by symbolic pictures - whether they are from the sphere of a pleasant natural ambience or from stunning spiritual ecstasy. All that glittering and bursting energy of words, verses, stanzas, songs and dramatical poems is directed towards the essentially simple point of the entire work, which is clearly expressed and which achieves an open communication with the reader, i.e., projected audience before whom actors come to stage - acting themselves - therefore, because Mirsad Solakovic's acting is inseparable from his poetry. Due to the artistic affinity and the humane vision of the author, the book "The Boy Who Said Nothing" becomes a segment of the project with unimagined manifestations - through words and motions, music and scene, all of which then melts into moving pictures of a film.

Publishing this book of poetry by Mirsad Solakovic, known abroad as a British actor of Bosnian origin, in a bilingual edition - in Bosnian and in English language - is of remarkable importance for the Diaspora People in the World and for the motherland, because the cultural bridges, which ennoble nations and states, creating a better World, befitting the humane humanbeing, continue to be built.

Sarajevo, 4/3/2016
Ibrahim Osmanbasic

Printed in Great Britain
by Amazon